35 Tips for Writing Powerful Prose Poems

35 Tips for Writing Powerful Prose Poems

Kaye D. Linden

ISBN: 1546414290
ISBN 13: 9781546414292

Dedicated to those who yearn to understand the playful prose poem.

Please visit me at www.kayelinden.com or email me at kaye@kayelinden.com

Acknowledgements:

Thank you to the talented authors of *The Bacopa Literary Review* 2016 who so generously allowed their prose poems, or parts thereof, to be included in this text:

Tina Barry
Sheryl Clough
Leslie Anne Mcilroy
Shannon Nakai
Marian Shapiro
Jacob Trask
Laura Madeline Wiseman

Thank you to Catherine Rankovic, my editor, to the Writers Alliance of Gainesville, Florida and to *The Bacopa Literary Review* editorial team for their continued support.

Prose poems are pure creation, the playful and daring edge of poetry. The writer provides powerful language and, above all, a truthful voice.

Table of Contents

Introduction

THIS BOOK ADDRESSES THE BEGINNING, intermediate or advanced writer of any age or grade level who desires to understand and write prose poetry. I hope that the interested writer will learn to love writing and exploring this liberating genre.

As poetry editor for *The Bacopa Literary Review*, I have edited over a thousand poetry submissions and read many prose poems that required only minor revisions or a little guidance to become publishable. Most of the insights in this book apply to great writing in general. I have focused the text on prose poems, popular with writers because of their unlimited potential for playful creativity. I invite you to accompany me through each chapter and prompt, to understand the spirit of this intriguing form. If you follow the step-by-step process of learning, you will have written several prose poems of your own by the end of the book.

This is the second reference book in the *35 Tips* series. These little books include only the essence, the facts, the bottom line. This textbook focuses on two essential qualities of great prose poetry: **brevity and specifics**.

LEARNING OBJECTIVES
The writer will:

* learn to **recognize** a prose poem
* learn to **understand** prose poems
* learn the **best techniques** for writing a prose poem
* **draft** several prose poems from prompts
* **revise** and polish these prose poems
* practice the **craft** of writing prose poems
* use the **resource list** for further exploration of prose poetry

CHAPTER 1

The prose poem

IF YOU LOVE ECCENTRIC, BEAUTIFUL things, you will enjoy prose poetry.

Here are **tips** about prose poetry:

a. Prose poetry speaks about the **truth** of the world as the poet sees it.

b. Poetry should be **clear**, understandable and make sense. Otherwise, poems are just words splashed on paper.

c. Writers of prose poems do not usually use the rhymes, rhythms and line breaks of **traditional** poetry.

d. In prose poetry, **each word** chosen is important.

e. Prose poetry skillfully uses **language** that inspires the reader.

f. Prose poets hope to amaze and **delight**.

g. Prose poetry might suggest its meaning with poetic language such as **metaphors or similes**.

h. Writers of prose poems concentrate on **scenes, description and surprise**.

i. Prose poetry can have a story line, but does **not need a story line**.

j. Prose poetry has **a center of gravity** the way the earth has a molten core.

k. Prose poets aim to arouse an **emotional response** in the reader.
l. Prose poetry can consist of two lines, or a **few paragraphs,** or longer.
m. Prose poetry includes **full sentences**.
n. Prose poetry has **a narrative shape** on the page: a sentence, a few sentences, a paragraph. That's one reason it is called "prose" poetry, because it is written in the shape of **prose.**
o. Writers should **read** their prose poems **aloud** because this is the best way to hear mistakes, catch skips in rhythm or meaning, inconsistencies, check the pacing and tense, or identify shifts in point of view.

Here's the first stanza from the prose poem "Big Bang" by Leslie Anne Mcilroy, published in *The Bacopa Literary Review* 2016:

Date with Syzygy

More than once, the sun and the moon doing things they've never, trading light for dark, all eclipse and aerial acrobatics. The stars, blinking with confusion, bumping into clouds in broad daylight, dawn and dusk dancing in drag, roosters crowing at twilight, and me, here at the window, waiting for a universe.

Prose poems and the beginning prose poem writer

A prose poem format offers the beginning writer a fantastic trampoline to bounce around creativity. A prose poem can be about any subject. The following chapters will help you write without rambling, choosing words and images that will move your readers. Many a beginning poet has broken through their self-doubt via this pathway. It is a lot of fun, but stick to the tips and suggestions until you have read and written lots of poems.

Don't bend the rules until you know them.

At the end of the book is a list of resources to inspire the beginner and excite the seasoned writer.

CHAPTER 2

Starting a prose poem

HERE IS A **PROMPT** TO get you started. What is a prompt?

A prompt is a suggestion that encourages the imagination.

After writing this draft of a "prose poem" you will have a beginning poem from which to work. With this, you can apply the tips and prompts in the rest of the book and write more prose poems. Remember to write in sentences, without broken lines, in paragraph style.

PROMPT:

a. In one long sentence, write a poem about a wild ride. For example, write about any of the following: riding a wild horse, a motorcycle, mountain bike, driving a car without brakes, going downhill, or riding an ostrich (now, that's a wild ride and I've done it!). You can go to the limits of your imagination. Remember, write it in one long sentence.

b. Now rewrite the same poem in more than one sentence and insert other words and descriptions.

c. Compare the two poems by reading them aloud and see which you prefer.

(Notice that breaking the poem into several sentences has the effect of slowing down the pace or speed of the poem.)

CHAPTER 3

The first few lines

THE FIRST FEW LINES OF a prose poem, after the title, are the most important lines. They draw the reader into the poem—or they might not. Will your reader keep reading? Begin with a fabulous or riveting statement:

> "A fractured blood moon peers through winter's pale dead branches, red cardinals feed their young munched-up seed from the unsquirrel-proof squirrel-proof birdfeeder, but the world tonight turns upside down and my hair doesn't even stand on end."

Do you want to keep reading? If the answer is "yes," then this line worked. Or not. Ask yourself why you would want to keep reading or why you would not want to keep reading.

PROMPT:

Begin with a simple sentence about what you might come across on a walk. For example, "In Alice's summer garden, waving green fern fronds gather around a cool, clear pond of splashing koi fish."

The **"picture"** created here is a nature **scene**. The reader understands that the scene includes a breeze or wind, movement, living fish, healthy green plants, a fertile garden, warmth, perhaps heat, probably a sunny day, the suggestion of a girl or woman by the name of Alice and a contrasting sense of coolness and clarity from the pond water. These suggestions and details conjure up a picture or **image** in the reader's mind.

NOW IT'S YOUR TURN.

Imagine yourself walking on a remote or busy beach, hiking alone in the mountains, walking on a suburban street or in a large city scuttling in between traffic, speed-walking a marathon, or jogging around a ship's deck. Write in **one sentence** about what you **see, hear, feel, smell, touch.**

CHAPTER 4

How long should it be?

PROSE POEMS CAN BE ANY length, even as long as a book. Most are a few paragraphs long or just a few sentences. To begin with, work on writing prose poems of one or two paragraphs, with each paragraph consisting of two or three sentences. After you are practiced and comfortable, you can write longer prose poems. Or you can write shorter ones. Writing very short prose poems takes as much work and skill as writing a long one.

PROMPT:

What would you like to write about?

Start with tiny steps of **one sentence at a time** and build on the first line until you have a paragraph.

Take the sentence you wrote in chapter three about walking, and add another few words. If you can, write another sentence about the first sentence.

Write about life

POETRY IS LANGUAGE UNDER PRESSURE. Poetry is language that has a job to do. Its job is to write about life. Look around you. Look out the window. Down the street. At the doctor's office. In the hospital. Across the field. In the sky. Inside the tunnel. Around the corner. At the airport. On the plane. (Look at that old man with the crazy orange hat turned upside down and sideways on his shoulder-length white hair.)

Sit still and listen.

What do you see? Hear? Feel? Smell? Taste? Sense?

That's life. That's what you will write about.

Writing in poetry means choosing **meaningful** words that do the job of **painting a picture** in the reader's mind.

Here's an example of how words **paint pictures** in the reader's mind:

Autumn—
Six-foot sunflowers crowd the fallowed fields with thousands
of seeded faces that turn together towards the sun in noon
heat, a chorus of yellow heads swaying farewell to summer.

Can you "see" this scene in your mind? Poets call an interior picture like this an "**image**."

CHAPTER 6

Other ways to paint pictures with words

"WORD WEIGHT" REFERS TO THE significance of each word used in the poem. How much meaning does the word offer the reader? For example, each word in the following phrase contributes to the over-all weight or intent of the following simile: *fluttering like a baby's heart.* Or consider Dr. Martin Luther King Jr.'s biblical simile from his **"I Have a Dream" speech:** "*. . .and will not be satisfied until justice rolls down like water and righteousness like a mighty stream.*"

Similes create inner pictures we call images. Similes make a comparison between two things and are most often connected by the word "like," meaning "it resembles," or the word "as."

Here are a few examples of similes:

a. The sunflower bent its head like a sad child.
b. She was tough as a diamond.
c. He acts like a bull in the courtroom.
d. The orange tasted like sweet fruit wine.

Dr. Martin Luther King Jr. joined the words "justice" and "righteousness," concepts we cannot see, with flowing water and a mighty stream, things we can see or feel. By joining words with actual things, he painted a vivid, realistic image in our minds that is still remembered decades later.

He could have said instead, "Let justice and righteousness prevail," and that is the same message, but its words are not as memorable. His memorable sentence used two similes:

"Let justice roll down LIKE water, and righteousness LIKE a mighty stream."

Try writing some similes. The more original, the better. Here are some prompts for you to fill in the blanks:

He laughed like a _____

The burnt barbecue tasted like _____

This perfume smells like _____

Having enough money is like _____

Sailing a rough ocean is like _____

If we say the object actually *is* another thing, then we are using **metaphor,** which is one of the most commonly used figures of speech in poetry. For example:

* He's a prince among men.
* The tattoo is a web over his body.
* All the world's a stage.
* He is a bull in the courtroom.

The metaphor changes the picture in the reader's mind. That is how it differs from a simile. For example, the simile "he is as stubborn as a donkey" becomes comical if we use the metaphor "he is a donkey."

To intensify your poem even more, include details from some of the five senses. Look at the difference from the first sentence below and the second sentence. The second sentence has only a few more words, but the picture painted is more intense.

1. Santa's sixteen secret elves crowded the living room and sang "Rudolph the Red-Nosed Reindeer" as their nimble fingers decorated tiny robes with silver stitches.
2. Santa's sixteen secret elves crowded the pine-scented living room and sang "Rudolph the Red-Nosed Reindeer" as their nimble little fingers decorated tiny green velvet robes with silver stitches.

Adding detail that describes the five senses is called "sensory detail."

CHAPTER 7

The creative process (drafting two poems)

LOOK AT THE SENTENCE YOU wrote in chapter two about a wild ride. Read this sentence aloud. Ask yourself the following questions:

a. Does the sentence make sense?
b. Does it paint a picture in your mind?
c. Can you see, hear, feel, taste what the sentence describes?
d. Are there words that seem like excess baggage?
e. Could you have chosen other words that might help paint a clearer, more sensory picture?

Choose **one** of the following prompts for your second prose poem:

a. You walk up to a house at night thinking your friend lives there, but the house is dark and the curtains are closed. Classical music plays from within the house. Do you ring the doorbell, or watch and wait? What thoughts race through your mind? Take us into the scene with your words. Write one or two paragraphs.

b. You see a woman in a wedding dress. She is standing alone on the beach holding only one silver shoe. Invent something strange about her. Maybe the hem of her dress has unraveled or an ink stain spatters the front of her dress. Maybe a cockatoo sits on her shoulder. Write one paragraph about her.

CHAPTER 8

Drafting and Crafting

It is time to work on the chosen poems that you have **drafted**. Choose any of the sentences or paragraphs you have written so far, and do the following to **craft** or hone the poem. At this point, choose only **one** poem to work on so you get practice in crafting.

In this chapter, you will follow the first two keys of revision: **cutting** and **organizing**.

Cut unnecessary words. Cutting means deleting words that don't mean anything, don't add to the poem, sound awkward, or are fillers not related to the point of your prose poem.

Read the following aloud as examples of cutting:

a. The immensely big, red sun finally sank down behind the very straight horizon. He climbed very slowly up to the island's tallest peak and quietly admired the calm blue ocean water surrounding the straight-edged, chalky-white rough cliffs of the rock-strewn mountains. At nightfall, he felt really tired, and so retreated into his cave and prepared to sleep.

HERE'S THE REVISED VERSION:

b. The red sun slipped behind the horizon. He climbed to the island's highest peak and admired the calm blue ocean surrounding the chalk-white cliffs of the rock-strewn mountains. At nightfall, he retreated to his cave and prepared to sleep.

Can you see where changes were made and understand why?

Does the second passage sound **clearer, tighter**? It was cut from 58 words to 40 words.

Did you notice the unintentional tongue twister? "The red sun sank." To fix the tongue twister, substitute a different word, such as "dropped," for "sank."

Comb through the first and second examples, and highlight where the changes were made.

Always **read your writing aloud** to hear whether a word is excessive, to hear mistakes, to hear an irregular beat or awkward rhythm, difficult words or unintentional tongue twisters. This is especially important in poetry. Prose poems are often short, but whether long or short, they must be concise.

ORGANIZE

Does the poem sound better and better with each cut and revision? Does each sentence build on the one before and expand the image for the reader? Is the progression logical?

These are your goals. Keep working on the poem until it sounds better to you.

ADD

Sometimes during revision, when worried about "the rules," poets might cut or trim a poem so closely that they drain all the life and texture out of their poem. Sometimes a poem might not seem finished even to the poet because it does not reach a conclusion or a high level of drama, conflict, description or emotion. In the rewriting stage, add to the poem what you think it needs.

PROMPT:

Examine a poem or narrative you have written or are in the process of writing. Highlight in yellow those words you can eliminate. Highlight in green the places you think the poem could use more description or sensory detail, or a simile or metaphor. You do not have to "explain" things to the reader, but the poem ought to be clear and logical in its progression of time and events. Now, rewrite the poem and read it aloud. How do you like it now?

CHAPTER 9

Prompts and more prompts

THIS CHAPTER WILL INSPIRE YOU to create more prose poems.

Write one paragraph using the following prompt as a jumping-off point. Write what crosses your mind and don't stop to judge what you are writing. This is a first draft. Later, you can look harder at what you wrote and improve it. For now, simply write and enjoy the process!

Do each one of these prompts:

1. **Write** a prose poem or a paragraph based on the theme "a bag of bones." Put on a timer for ten minutes and write freely.

THEN:

2. **Read** what you just wrote. Think about what you would do with a bag of bones. What might a dog do with it? What if bones were the local currency? What if you found a bag of bones in your backyard? Now rewrite, using what you've imagined, and **remember to use the five senses.** What do those bones feel like? Sound like? Look like? Do they smell? What kind of bag are they in?

Sensory words and images appeal to our sense of smell, taste, sight, hearing and psyche. They give the poem extra dimensions that make it powerful and more like reality.

Review what you have written. Read it aloud to hear how it sounds.

3. **Repetition** is a valuable tool in prose poetry if it is not over-done. In one of the paragraphs you have written, consider where repetition (as in "drip, dripping") might work.

4. Go back over one paragraph and highlight the following words:

   "is," "was," "are," "be," "would be," "had." Rewrite sentences and cut these words. Use **meaningful** words to replace them, or rephrase the sentence.

5. Take one of the paragraphs and write it backwards. This helps the poet to "see" outside his or her comfort zone. Does it prompt any ideas?

6. Write a paragraph about someone's laughter. What does the laughter suggest? Will your paragraph convey anger, ridicule, joy?

7. Choose a topic and write a paragraph starting with a long sentence. Then write a short sentence. Keep alternating between a long and short sentence until the poem feels finished.

8. Choose a topic and write a poem in one very long sentence of close to a paragraph length. If you are having trouble thinking of a topic, open a dictionary and close your eyes. Circle your finger and randomly pick a word or three words. Open your eyes and let that word or words lead you into a poem.

9. Stand up in a room by yourself and read the poem aloud. Listen to how it sounds. Where can you take a breath, pause and emphasize the next word? Read it aloud again.

Reading aloud becomes easier with practice and reading in public, as scary as it appears, does get easier the more you do it.

10. Whatever you write, try writing as honestly and truthfully as you can. These are **first drafts**. Keep them to review and rewrite later.

Writing a paragraph is not the same thing as writing a crafted prose poem. Writing a paragraph is a beginning step towards writing a prose poem, but it must also incorporate the elements of language and skill that define it as a prose poem. Bear this in mind as you study this book and use the five prompts below.

PROMPT 1:
Copy and read a prose poem or one of the sample pieces in the text and stay aware of how it makes you feel. Examine these pieces closely and highlight the words or devices (poetic tricks or language, such as similes or sensory detail) that made you feel this way.

PROMPT 2:
Write a paragraph that includes these words: starfish, stranger, highway.

PROMPT 3:
Write a paragraph using these words: oranges, barrels, monkeys.

PROMPT 4:

Look in the mirror. Describe your eye color using a simile, and write a prose poem about how people with your eye color "see" the world.

PROMPT 5:

You are volunteering in a remote village in the Himalayas where technology does not exist. There are no cellphones, telephone connections, newspapers, televisions or radios. Describe a person who lives in this village and what he or she looks like. What does he or she wear, eat, do for work and recreation? Keep the description to two paragraphs.

CHAPTER 10

Who is your audience?

THE READER IS YOUR AUDIENCE.

Who do you write for? Yourself, your reader, or both?

I write for both. Creative writing is above all, **communication.**
Communication must be clear, so your poem must be clear.

Assume that your readership might include an eleven-year-old boy in Chicago reading his first prose poem, a woman in Rio de Janeiro, a graduate student who has come to the USA from the Philippines to study, a soldier who is ten thousand miles from home and reads poetry when he or she is not on duty, a group of patients in a nursing home, a fifty-five-year-old in a refugee tent, or a group of writers working to improve their understanding of prose poetry. Write your poem so that all these people will understand it and feel a response. Write it well so that the majority of readers will think that reading it was worth their while.

No matter who your reader is, he or she hopes that a poem will provide a new or interesting experience. The following are not prose poems, but well-known regular poems, which will demonstrate how to trigger a response in the reader:

Google and read Maya Angelou's poem "Phenomenal Woman." How does it make you feel? Angelou wanted the reader to feel emotion during and after reading her poem. She successfully transferred this emotion through the poem to you, the reader. That takes skill and practice. Can you identify how she did this?

Read Robert Frost's "Stopping by Woods on a Snowy Evening" and notice how the poet makes the reader feel present in the scene. How did Frost's choice of words and images make this illusion happen?

Keep the reader involved in the poem by choosing a fresh subject or point of view. Whatever the poem says, the poem must be clear. **When in doubt, keep it simple.**

What experience do you want your reader to have? Do you want to share an insight?

Do you want your reader to feel a specific emotion such as sadness, affirmation, reverence or joy? Through **carefully chosen language**, your prose poem can be clear and concise.

CHAPTER 11

Not enough information

NEW WRITERS OF PROSE POEMS tend to hesitate and under-write. They have trouble coming up with ideas and are afraid to write down or share their ideas after they have them. Part of the problem is lack of confidence, which comes from fear of criticism. After you have worked through this text, you will have learned valuable writing skills, as well as created and revised several poems. This will give you the confidence to write more without rambling.

Write about what you love in this world, and when you are writing a first draft, avoid criticizing or judging what you are writing down. The best way to do this is to turn on a timer (around ten minutes) and write without stopping. You can always revise and hone this first draft later. Creative writing is a layered process. It's not "one and done." Poets might rewrite a poem a dozen times until it communicates exactly what they want it to in concise language.

❀ PROMPT:
Open any book at a random page with your eyes closed. Circle your finger and let it land on one word and write it down. Do the same thing two other times for a total of three times. Now, set the timer for ten minutes and combine these

words into a scene with description, using all five senses. Write with abandon, not stopping to judge or change anything. Forget about proper punctuation for now; you can correct that later.

CHAPTER 12

Too much information

ASSUME THE READER IS HIGHLY intelligent but doesn't want to work too hard to understand your poem. Don't beat him or her over the head about your beliefs or that "life is hard and we die in the end." Create something new or create a fresh perspective on an old theme. Don't tell the reader the "winter was cold." Instead, offer the **image** of a woman "rubbing pale fingers and blowing hot breath across her hands." This is the difference between "telling" the reader your truth and "demonstrating" or "showing" it through visual language.

Be careful about using graphic, gory images. A poem must do more than shock people.

Write all the poems you want about how you have been mal-treated or betrayed, or how sad you are, but don't expect people or publishers to be interested in reading these poems. Because every-one can tell horror stories about their lives and everyone has had a death in the family, it is unlikely that you will come up with a new and fresh poem about abuse, victimization, illness, hospitalization, or about a relative's dying.

In addition to under-writing, new writers of prose poetry might write too much because writing "tight," or with just the right number of meaningful words that **show** a picture, is a learned skill. The result of writing too much is confused or rambling writing that has lost its center of gravity and wanders without focus. Too many words create awkward sentences, or even chronological inconsistency. They overwhelm the reader who becomes lost in the prose. **Clear writing is paramount in all writing.** Writing is about communication. Can you understand a garbled phone message, or would you want it to be clear?

Following the tips in this text will enable you to learn the skills needed to write enough without writing too much. It will offer the skills needed to achieve clear, concise writing. Practicing these skills leads to excellence.

Here is an example of too much information:

After three more very long days of needed rest inside his now very familiar cave home, after such a long, long journey, Prasanga climbed slowly once more to the highest, tallest peak of the lone island and enthusiastically watched the beautiful summer evening descend over the ocean's blue waters even though he felt tired. He thought about his past and the many years he spent underground without a sky or without the stars. He had never seen anything like the sky or the stars and had known only the blackness of the darkness. Even his father had never seen the sky or the stars. The other tribespeople had not either. They would have been fascinated by what he saw now. He wished they were here and remembered his childhood. White lightning skipped and raced across the very heated skies and the colored stars of the legendary Southern Cross sparkled magically against a scarlet evening backdrop.

Here's one alternative to so much information:

After three days of rest inside his now familiar cave home, Prasanga climbed once more to the tallest peak of the island

and watched the evening descend. White lightning skipped across heated skies and stars of the legendary Southern Cross sparkled against a scarlet evening backdrop.

In the second example, the scene is focused and the image clear. In the first example, the extra words and information weigh down the scene and we get lost in the extra information.

PROMPT:
Examine a piece you just wrote and read it aloud. What can you cut or trim that will tighten the writing? Revise the writing with what you now know.

CHAPTER 13

Naming your poems

THE READER FIRST NOTICES THE title of your poem. Based on the title, the reader decides whether he or she feels intrigued enough to continue reading the poem.

When a reader feels intrigued enough to continue reading, you have "hooked" his or her interest and attention. It is like tasting a new food. Based on the first taste, you decide whether to eat more.

A title is not just a word or two patched onto the top of a poem. Poem titles, like song titles or book titles, need to be creative and unique to attract a reader's attention. It takes time to create a unique title. Here are a few tips on choosing a title:

a. Avoid one-word titles such as "Springtime," or "Love." They have been used so many times that they are worn out and not unique.

b. Avoid titles that begin with "My." Seeing a poem titled "My Dog," the reader instantly gets the message that the poem was written for the poet and his dog and for no one else. The reader will feel shut out by the title and probably won't read the poem. The effort you expended to write a good poem and move a reader's heart is therefore wasted—merely because the title is not right. Change the title. "Try titles on" your poem as you would try on clothes, looking for something a little different and eye-catching. For example, rather than "My Dog," write "That Black Dog with the White Eye Patch Plays Pretty" or "A Labrador Named Eddie."

c. Always title every poem, even if it's a temporary title. "Untitled" is not an option.

The writing and inventiveness in a title will reflect the writing in the poem.

Which in the following pairs of poem titles is more intriguing?

* "Camping"
* "Sleeping Unsafe at Camp Wilderness"
* "Woman in the Wind"
* "Woman Blooming for the Wind Machine"

What do you "see" when you look at these titles? What picture does each one paint in your mind?

The title is the first contact between your poem and its reader. Do not be afraid to "try on" different titles for your poem or change your title five or six times. Writing titles is part of the creative process, so be creative! Hook the reader's attention with an interesting title and make that first contact count.

PROMPT:
Study the following titles:

* "Boneheaded"
* "Perfect Body in One Sentence"

* "The Linear and Circular One Sentence of Tattoo Designs Over His Body"
* "The Wet"
* "Infusion Profusion"
* "Death Came to Me with Soft Fingers"

How do you respond to or feel about each of the above titles? Write down two **images** that arise in your mind from each title.

If a title doesn't seem quite right, use the dictionary and thesaurus to find words that might be creative alternatives. *Webster's New Roget's A-Z Thesaurus* sits next to me like a faithful puppy.

Prompt:
Again, circle your finger around a page of a magazine or newspaper, and pick out three or four random words. Use them (and any other words you need) to write an exciting title for a poem.

Now that you have the title, write a prose poem for it.

CHAPTER 14

Point of view

"I," "You," or "We"?

WHAT IS POINT OF VIEW in a poem?

If the poem is written from the perspective of its author or the narrator, using the word "I," then the poem has a first-person point of view. If the poem is addressed to a "you," it is written in the second-person point of view. If the poem is about "he" or "she" or someone with a name, it is written in the third-person point of view.

The "I" in a poem is not necessarily the poet speaking. The "I" can be any character in the poet's imagination. A jungle character might speak about his or her life in the jungle, hiding from the hunter's gun, sleeping in treetops at night. Keep in mind that an "I" in a poem is the speaker or narrator of the poem, and not necessarily the poet.

If you can write only poems about yourself or from only one point of view, your poetic horizons will be quite limited. Use your imagination!

Addressing a poem to a "you," especially if the poet really means "I" or "he" or "she," gives the reader incorrect, imprecise information.

"You" becomes annoying if repeated during a prose poem. As readers, we don't take issue with first-person or third-person viewpoints repeated, because they sink below our awareness. However, second person can sound awkward. If a poem sounds awkward, the viewpoint might be one reason.

EXAMPLES OF WHAT'S WRONG WITH USING SECOND-PERSON POINT OF VIEW:

* "You walked me down the aisle," could mean either "My father walked me down the aisle, and this poem is for my father to read" or "You, the reader, walked me down the aisle." The meaning is not clear.
* "Grandma, you loved chocolates in heart-shaped boxes," sounds like a line from a poem written to the poet's grandmother. That is fine, but please understand that readers, including publishers, have little interest in a poem obviously written for only one person to read. This use of "you" shuts the reader out.
* Write "I" if you really mean "I." No one is fooled when a poet uses the second person point of view to describe personal experience. "You were swallowed up in popularity contests you never won" should be written as "I was swallowed up in popularity contests I never won." Be honest when speaking as yourself and don't hide the truth behind a "you."

Choose an interesting point of view and whichever one you choose, stay with it.

How do you want the reader to hear the poem? From which viewpoint or angle? From whose perspective? I, we, you, it, he, she, they?

Consider using "we" which is the first-person **plural.** It's fun and includes the reader as part of the "we." Using "we" captures much more universal significance and embracing of the reader than does "you." "We" adds a sense of curiosity. Who is the "we?" Are they members of a tour group? Two sisters traveling together? Using "we" can create a sense of intrigue.

Here is an excerpt using "we" from *Tales from Ma's Watering Hole:*

> We were there when the girl from Sydney drowned in the desert. We warned her. She didn't listen to stories of light-ning gods who jump from sunny skies. Sydney girl took to the red sands alone, in the afternoon heat, unsoiled backpack, Australian flag blowing around on a stick. She wore shorts. We watched the spikey mulga scratch her legs bloody till we couldn't see her any more. Yes, we warned her alright, we old women. She was fooled by our far-away eyes, stained teeth and chewing-tobacco lips that formed words she didn't want to hear.

Prompt: Set a timer for fifteen minutes and draft a prose poem starting with the word "We." Don't stop to edit or judge. Just write.

PROMPT:
Write a poem from the perspective of a woman or man singing to a rowdy audience, or trying to keep up with a difficult exercise class, or an athlete running a marathon.

CHAPTER 15

To use punctuation or not?

PUNCTUATION IS YOUR VOICE COMMUNICATING through the written word. It lets the reader know where you might pause or take a breath, where to emphasize a word or phrase and to accent the rhythm, the music and pacing of your speaking voice. That is one reason to read your poem aloud—to hear how the sentences flow, their rhythm and if the punctuation needs changing. For example, if you ask a question, the reader won't know it's a question unless there is a question mark at the end of the sentence to indicate a rise in the voice. Without the question mark, the sentence stays flat—a statement.

Say these aloud:

"Did you say nonsense?" He shrugged his shoulders and left the room.
"Nonsense," he said, on his way out of the room.

The most effective way of writing or speaking with emphasis and rhythm is with the use of the **pause**. In speaking, we use our breath and the space of time. In writing, we use commas, periods, dashes and other **punctuation** to mark those pauses.

Excluding punctuation in prose poetry does not make it radical or more powerful, but rather the opposite. It can be harder for a reader to understand. The harder the poem is to understand, the fewer readers it will have. There will always be some readers who will think a poem is not punctuated because the poet is ignorant or was afraid of punctuating incorrectly.

In the beginning, always use punctuation unless you are playing around.

At the same time, beware of overusing punctuation marks. One exclamation mark in a poem may be more than enough, and a variety of sentence lengths and punctuation offers interest to your writing. Write what you love and with passion and the voice will sing through the poem.

Prose poems are about stirring an emotional response in the reader. To do that, the poet must care about the subject of the poem and want to communicate to others so they too will care or at least be interested. Whichever way the poet decides to go, the crucial aspect of writing prose poetry is that a poem has structure. The structure of a poem is like the bones upon which the writer builds the flesh or the substance of the poem. Structure includes well-placed and meaningful language and punctuation.

CHAPTER 16

Unity

UNITY MEANS KEEPING THE INDIVIDUAL piece of writing focused on the same theme. Don't write about cows and then go on a tangent about the newly discovered planets of the solar system.

PROPORTION

Proportion refers to the sense of balance of the poem, its beginning leading to a solid and meaningful middle and an ending that makes the poem feel complete.

If what happens in the poem should be told chronologically but its order is skewed or out of sequence, the poem will dissolve into pieces that don't fit together. The reader will become disoriented as to the poem's setting in time and place. When in doubt, use chronological order for the events in your poem. That's the best way to keep a reader from being confused.

PROMPT:

Write a paragraph or a poem going backwards in time.
  For example, you can use this prompt:

You meet your lover in a remote hole-in-the-wall cafe, but halfway through the romantic meeting, his wife or her husband walks in. You didn't know he or she had a spouse.

(Or, *your* husband or wife walks in.)

Go backwards beginning at the ending. Write the last line first and continue backwards in time, sentence by sentence.

The prose must "hang together" as a **satisfactory whole.** If the poem sounds confusing or awkward, rewrite it. If someone else reads it and doesn't understand the poem, ask them to offer you specific reasons as to why they don't understand the poem and then rewrite it.

CHAPTER 17

Using tenses

TENSE IN THE ENGLISH LANGUAGE refers to whether an action occurred in the present or the past or will occur in the future. For example, he "ate." This example is known as a past tense. Other tenses are much more complicated and might include "had," "have," "will have," "must have been," and so on, and that is all you need to know right now. Let's keep it simple!

Here are examples:

Past tense: she sang, she sung, she laughed, he ate, he cut
Present tense: she sings, she laughs, he eats, he cuts
Future tense: she will sing, she will laugh, he will eat, he will cut

Then, there are the variations such as "she had sung," "she has sung," "she will have sung," "he would have sung," "he should have sung," "he could have sung"—can, shall, may, might, must sing. Phew! Here's my advice: Leave out those variations in your poems and keep the tense simple and **active** as in the examples for past, present and future tense above. Avoid the verbs from the "to be" family, such as "is" or "was."

PROMPT:

Write a prose poem in the past tense. Then write the same poem in the present tense. What is the difference?

(Answer: Present tense brings more of a sense of *intimacy* and *immediacy* than past tense. One major impact of present tense is that it speeds up the pacing and implies a sense of urgency.)

PROMPT:

Rewrite one of your poems from the past or present tense into the future tense.

Or from the future tense into the present or past tense.

Here's an example from "When Songbirds Take Flight" by Shannon Nakai:

Present tense:

Dorothy presses her wide barreled thumbs along the fluted rims of pie crust. Her eyes, the color of rain, follow the grease-smocked recipe. She sprinkles fistfuls of flour on to the counter. Outside Aunt Em scatters seeds for the chickens, watching the girl in the window frame.

Past tense:

Dorothy pressed her wide barreled thumbs along the fluted rims of pie crust. Her eyes, the color of rain, followed the grease-smocked recipe. She sprinkled fistfuls of flour on to the counter. Outside Aunt Em scattered seeds for the chickens, and watched the girl in the window frame.

Future tense:

> Dorothy will press her wide barreled thumbs along the fluted rims of pie crust. Her eyes, the color of rain, will follow the grease-smocked recipe. She will sprinkle fistfuls of flour on to the counter. Outside Aunt Em will scatter seeds for the chickens, and will watch the girl in the window frame.

Which tense grabs you most? Consider rewriting poems in different tenses to express a different meaning. Play with the effect each tense gives. In the above example, the future tense "will" distracts the reader because the word "will" occurs too often. By contrast, readers hardly notice the present or past tenses. That is why they're the most commonly used.

Read the above examples aloud and listen to how each tense changes the **mood** or feeling. In addition, note how the past tense reads similarly to the present tense, but the future tense sounds like a list of commands.

CHAPTER 18

Make the poem active and alive

ACTIVE AND PASSIVE VOICE

DID YOU EVER HEAR A teacher say, "Take the sentence out of the passive voice and rewrite it in the active voice?" This is a concern when you are rewriting a poem and trying to make it more alive and vivid.

Passive and **active** sentences have nothing to do with a sentence's content. "Passive" and "active" are about verb usage.

Active sentences contribute to excellent, tight writing. Passive sentences drag down and slow down the reader, interfere with rhythm and pacing, and create distance and an awkward read.

> a. **Passive**: His bruised body **was crushed** by the watery centrifuge, and one limb at a time **was twisted** by **the raging currents** of the flooding Mississippi.
>
> b. **Active: The raging currents** of the flooding Mississippi, a watery centrifuge, **crushed** (verb) his bruised body and **twisted** (verb) each limb, one at a time.

a. **Passive:** The screaming woman **had been besieged** by floodwaters and **was being pulled** down.

b. **Active: Floodwaters besieged** (verb) the screaming woman, **pulling** (verb) her down.

In the above examples, the **subject "The raging currents"** in the first active example and the **"floodwaters"** in the second active example are the **subjects of the action verb, meaning they are the things doing the action.**

In the passive examples, the man and then the screaming woman are crushed, besieged, pulled down. This makes the sentence **passive** because the action is **received** by the victim who is passively getting crushed or pulled down. The action is being done to the victim or receiver of the action.

This is a difficult concept to grasp but an important one.

THE KEY CONCEPT FOR YOU TO REMEMBER IS THE FOLLOWING:

<u>When writing prose poetry, use the active voice rather than the passive voice, unless there is a justifiable grammatical or logistical reason to use the passive voice.</u>

PROMPT:
Examine the poems you have written and highlight the passive voice if you used it.

Rewrite what you wrote into active voice.

Now, more on choosing verbs and understanding them:

Verbs from the "to be" family: Examples in sentences

It can <u>be</u> confusing.
I <u>am</u> alone. I <u>was</u> alone.
I <u>will have to be</u> alone.
You <u>used to be</u> home.
You <u>are</u> home.
She <u>is</u> singing. She <u>was</u> singing. She <u>will be</u> singing.
He is <u>being</u> rambunctious.
He <u>had</u> <u>to have been feeling</u> ill.
It has <u>been</u> confusing.
It <u>will be</u> confusing.

Stay away from the verb "to be" and its family when possible, especially in a short poem. Poems lose power with **excessive** use of "was," "were," "used to be," "would, have been" and so on as outlined above in the examples. Of course, exceptions to this rule exist, but if the poet must use "to be" verbs, keep them to a minimum. I am amazed at the repetition of these and other unweighted, colorless verbs in otherwise tight writing. They often appear in the first line, and repeat throughout the second and third lines. In a short piece, keep it tight by leaving the "to be" family of verbs and substituting verbs that are more descriptive.

Prompt: Write a prose poem about stones. In your first line use a simile. After that, simply write about stones and let the ideas you have about "stones" take you on a strange journey.

Prompt: Write about crossing a train track on foot at night. How does it feel? What do you smell, hear, see?

Prompt: Write about whatever you first see when you look out the window. Write one paragraph and stop. Do you feel as if you have more to say about this topic? If so, continue to write.

Review: Examine your work, read it aloud, and highlight the words that appeared to work well and those that could work better.

How might you **rewrite** your poems so that the words paint a more detailed picture?

Remember to use similes and metaphors if you are comfortable with them.

CHAPTER 19

Descriptive words

How many and which ones?

Adverbs, words that end in "ly," add meaning to a verb, and adjectives add meaning to a noun. For example:

John works **quickly**. "Quickly" is an adverb and describes the verb, "works." Adjectives add meaning to nouns. For example:

John has a **large** house. "Large" is an adjective and describes "house," which is a **noun**.

There are explanations and exceptions to general rules, of course, but for right now, you don't have to know the exceptions. Let's keep it simple:

Too many adverbs and adjectives weaken an otherwise powerful poem.

Use an adverb only when necessary. Instead of resorting to adverbs or excessive use of adjectives, consider writing to present an image or vision in the reader's head. Choose nouns that offer strong enough images so that adjectives might not be necessary.

Here is an example that uses just enough adjectives to paint a crisp, clear mental picture, not too few or too many. (By the way, ask yourself: What tense is it written in? What is the point of view?)

Underneath the massive willow tree in our backyard, hummingbirds hover over the white blooms of a strawberry patch I planted this spring. In the evenings, calmed by the sweet scent of hanging jasmine vines, we stroll the trail around our five acres and explore. In the far corners of the property we discovered rusting fence parts, bundles of chicken wire and hills of burnt firewood. The other day, while planting more strawberries near the willow tree, I uncovered two baby teeth, a thin silver bangle and a dusty gold ring wrapped inside a piece of ragged white silk.

In writing description, avoid tired and worn-out words or phrases such as "ruby red lips," "cold as ice," "shimmering moonlight," "blood red sun," "pretty as a picture" or "his eyes glazed over." These are boring expressions used so many times that they have lost their impact. They are called **clichés.**

PROMPT:
Highlight the adjectives in the above piece of writing and examine their necessity in the work. Do the same with one of the prose pieces you have written. Do the words create a picture in your head? If they do not cast an image, don't use them.

Delete your least favorite adjective from the poem. Chances are that the poem will be fine without it.

Next, highlight the clichés or worn-out phrases in your work. Think about another way of expressing what you mean. Can you come up with a refreshing or interesting combination of words or similes that will work well?

CHAPTER 20

An easy fix

WORDS THAT END IN "LY"

THE EASIEST AND MOST SIMPLE way to rein in a poem is by finding all the words that end in "**ly**" and cutting them out. Most adverbs end in "ly." These words slow down the writing and label the poem as that of an amateur writer. Even though an occasional adverb or two works well in creative pieces, as a general statement it can be said that the writing tightens up and sounds much clearer and focused without the adverbs. A pared-down, unencumbered poem will shine.

OTHER MODIFIERS:

Comb through your poems with a **keen eye** for expressions and words so familiar that you don't "hear" them anymore. These include clichés. Look closely at each adjective, adverb, expression and phrase and decide which words can be cut. Be aware of words or modifiers that are **redundant** or repeated twice. For example, "she whispered softly." The word "whispered" implies speaking softly, so "softly" is redundant. Or, a "terrible tragedy" where the word "tragedy" by itself implies "terrible." Other examples of old or redundant expressions are "two twins," "three triplets," "the morning after the day before," "nodded his head," "peace and quiet."

Here is an example of such expressions or excess wording:

> Firstly, let me tell you about the majority of people who ride on the cross-country fast express train. It's pretty noisy on that train where each and every mother is rocking and singing her baby to sleep or feeding a screaming, crying toddler. Precious and few are the moments of peace and quiet a passenger can get on this supposedly fast express train which really goes awfully slowly given that it arrives in a whole ten hours to its final destination, when by car it takes only two hours. It's basic and fundamental knowledge that riding by train is slower than riding by motor car but still, prior to and before cars, we had trains, and in this day and age, traveling by train on a regular basis avoids automobile fume pollution and traffic. So as to be able to go to work by train, one should have peace and quiet in order to have a time period in which to work. Above and beyond all that, if that's the case and you have to work on the train, don't travel by train at night when the commotion and noise are by far the loudest.

WHAT CAN YOU DISCOVER ON EXAMINING THE ABOVE PASSAGE?

Highlight the clichés, the unnecessary words and phrases that can benefit from tightening. Rewrite the passage by **cutting** as many words as you can without changing what is said.

Prompt:

Read through a poem you have written, highlighting the "ly" endings. Consider how you could revise the work to avoid most of these adverbs.

Read through another poem and highlight the expressions or phrases for which one word would suffice.

CHAPTER 21

Ending the poem/
the last few lines

END WITH A SPECIFIC IMAGE.

In prose poems, a satisfactory ending is achieved by either circling back to the beginning image of the first few lines or by closing with a specific image in the last few lines.

See how the images of tattoos and stories connect in the following example:

a. David runs through Goliath with a sword but Goliath stands strong, his sandal strap broken by the tip of steel, blood at the ankle, a few hairs shaved from his knee, but he stays upright, an angel of the bottomless pit, the hero of one **tattooed story** with its **swirly blue ink marks connecting letters** over each vertebra . . .

b. . . . and he dreads the time when he runs out **of tattoo space on his skin** and he must share his **stories with his words** instead.

PROMPT:

Connect the poem's opening image with its final image.

Write a prose poem beginning with the image of a whale on the beach and ending with an image of the whale now returned to the ocean, or another image of your choice that connects with the beginning one.

Write a prose poem about being released from a trap. Before writing, envision where or how you were trapped and finally freed. The trap image can flow into the freed image. Before writing, think: How does freedom after captivity feel? Experience that feeling for a few minutes. How were you released from the trap? Who else was there? Did this happen indoors or outdoors? What's next now that you are free?

CHAPTER 22

Examples of prose poems

Here are a few examples of prose poems for your examination. Most of these poems were accepted for publication in *The Bacopa Literary Review 2016*.

For more examples and further readings, there are references to prose poetry writers and collections in the resource list at the end of this book.

See which elements in the poems work, in your opinion, and which don't. Look at the tips you have studied so far and study the poems with those tips in mind.

Remember, liking a poem is a matter of **perspective**. What one person loves, another might disdain. Read these aloud and hear the different use of rhythm, words and poetic devices such as repetition and punctuation.

Poem one

When Songbirds Take Flight
by Shannon Nakai

The farmhouse, September 20, 1913, Elk County, KS
Dorothy presses her wide barreled thumbs along the fluted rims of piecrust. Her eyes the color of rain follow

the grease-smocked recipe. She sprinkles fistfuls of flour onto the counter. Outside Aunt Em scatters seeds for the chickens, watching the girl in the window frame. Her gaze follows Dorothy in the mornings when she wanders from room to room filling the vases with milkweeds and gold-enrods, when she gently lifts the never-played sheet music on the piano as if to sing. Dorothy tosses old tennis balls off the side of the barn; she sleeps in rose-colored sheets and hides her underwear stained with blood beneath a pil-lowcase stuffed with love notes from a boy at school. She does not know that Em has fingered these letters, dustpan and broom in hand, teetering with a newfound terror. Her little songbird, as she used to call her, is vanishing. No lon-ger planting kisses on the chicken eggs. No longer calling the pigs by name during the feeding. Once Dorothy dis-appeared for an entire day. Em found her starry-eyed on her back in a soy field, babbling about a faraway place and plans she had for returning there. When Em sobbed, she laughed; when Em whipped her, she sang. Dorothy drifts now away from the window, wiping the flour that rimes her fingers. Going where she pleases. Baking on a whim. Em has pleaded and wept and shattered glasses against the walls, but the girl's hardening face and softening limbs always retreat. She insists the faraway place is real, she insists that she is going back, restless in the real world, which she now calls the dream world, ready, she says, to wake up again.

POEM TWO

Splintered
by Jacob Trask

the crack   in the frame
is thin   almost non-existent
it runs   parallel
from top   peak
of jamb   too far
almost   impossibly
to the floor   it's in my head
only through   this determined
observation   *everything*
all of it   the thought of it even
has been found   scarred, maybe
deeply fractured   broken

POEM THREE

Non-Sense
by Marian Kaplan Shapiro

There's nothing to say about the green that hasn't been said before about the red the blue the yellow wallpaper peppered with cornflowers, the raspberries on the counter the coffee grinder set to espresso, the cabinets that whisperclose themselves sighing graciously on the cupsmugsglasses resting on their hooks and racks, the drawers of cookbooks, mildewed manuals, and long expired coupons, the knives of special shapes and sizes for the cuttingslicingdicing of the carrots celery mushrooms onions breads and (yes) the meats; the closet for the brooms the brushes sponges, brillo, all the soapspowders for the cleaningshining of the pots and plates and bowls and un-silverware, and what to say about the pre-smart fridge that cannot clean itself, or learn to scan the sell-by dates, issuing pithy action orders (toss the milk), channeling her twin sister Our Lady of the GPS (turn left on Main), there's nothing to say at all about the kitchen except that you like your coffee in the Eiffel tower mug.

CHAPTER 23

Are prose poems stories?

ALTHOUGH PROSE POEMS CAN SOMETIMES tell stories, prose poems are not stories.

A story is a **series of events** in which a character or characters undergo **conflict and change**. The driving force in a story is either an interesting **plot**, an interesting **character,** or both.

Poems can incorporate elements of story, as in the following example, but prose poems are mainly **driven by poetic language** and not by the plot or character. For example, note the repetition in the following prose poem and the emphasis on imagery and language. If I cut the repetition and tighten up language in the following, the story elements will emerge with more strength. I have boldfaced a few language examples that identify this piece as prose poetry rather than a story. Note the treatment of punctuation or lack of it and the rhythm and pacing that arises from the language used. The following poem has a frantic pace, partly because of the handling of punctuation and poetic devices such as repetition.

Example of a story in prose poetry:

The Wet
by Kaye Linden

Ma, aboriginal toothless shaman, throws her ninety-nine-year-old bones into the front seat of the windowless jeep and jams her foot down on the accelerator. Desert driving, flash flood driving with rising waters at the hubcaps and **trackless tires sinking fast into whirling mud swirls.** Sky blows blacker than her skin, wind whips red welts into her hanging jawline, Ma pains on, the falling down mulga-wood homestead in sight, too distant on the **boiling roiling** horizon, **straight one-line straight line straight ahead** no wavering but straight the shortest distance between two points. Rain **pouring pouring pouring torrential blinding into her old eyes she keeps driving driving driving through driving rain to get home home home before the rusty untrusty jeep** sinks deeper into sudden ravines and eddies that grow rounder and hungrier taking but seconds to fill holes in the ground. She reaches the **leaning splitting woodpile homestead in the raining pouring driving wet, the wet, the Alice Springs wet, the wet** that only those people who live in The Alice know, understand, and brace for every five years. The homestead swirls under water, **turning and topsy and turvy and upside down and inside out, her broken armchair floating in pieces, rusted pots afloat, the sheltie dog swimming to meet her, tongue lolly-gagging hello, eyes yellowed and alight, but Ma's jeep coughs and rattles and chokes** and sinks with Ma not a swimmer but a hiker with strong old hiking legs, army boots that anchor her down into water. She grabs the old dog's matted wet back and they both go down and around, thunder announcing

their pending demise, kookaburra laughter long gone**, gasping and hacking and face just up level with water, eyes turned up to the heavens,** to the ancient gods whose hands don't reach out. "Where are you, you bastards?" Ma shouts to the sky and the dog whines a **carping whittling fingernails-down-the blackboard kind of cry** that only those from The Alice understand, only those who have seen **white brittle bones bleached** in desert heat and sun after those on a run for their lives have lost. Panting dog and woman cling to each other, **going down, going down, going down but with a whoosh and a gurgle the water stops, the rain stops, the rivers cease running, the widening knife-like gaps** in red mud close and Ma stands on her feet again, holding the dog in her arms, sinking to ankles in army boots, but standing in remnants of a flash flood in Australian desert,
here now,
there now,
gone.

PROMPT:
Identify the story line or theme in the above poem.
    Rewrite it without the poetic language.
    How does it read now?
    Do you prefer one version over the other version? Why?
    Take a short story you have written, or a story you often tell, and turn it into a prose poem. Insert poetic imagery and language to make it a poem.

CHAPTER 24

Dialogue in prose poetry

Dialogue works well in prose poems if it is kept to a **minimum**. Monologue or "stream of consciousness" writing can use lengthy dialogue, but usually that works best in the initial draft and not as a final prose poem. Inserting a line or two of dialogue in prose poetry can work to support its theme. In the following examples, note the minimal use of dialogue.

Here's examples of how dialogue might work.

An extract from the fantasy "Under the Frankincense Trees" by Laura Madeline Wiseman.

When we arrive in this land of the Dragon, we don't know the trees, the burn of such heat, a place of no water. I set my tracker to map. You beat your hands. I carry the vials. You carry the food. Few visible creatures are among us—hikers, one man on a motorbike, a woman with a basket and an umbrella. The only noise is wind. I'm trying not to leave you. You're trying to steady your walk. In the silence, we study the bark of trees, the reach of limbs, the canopy cap—more bed of needles than leafy bough. *Do not climb*, you say, translating the signs in dragon tongue, another language you speak alone. People do. You drop our sacks and reach into the branches. I reach too. They feel like the veined hands of the very old. You lift yourself in and climb until you disappear. I collect our sacks and continue hiking. I pass more signs in dragon tongue. I pass more hikers, some with packs of monsters. From a fairy ring of trees at the edge of the valley, I see them. Trolls pace in circles, arms above their heads swaying. Some wear chains. Some groan. Some shake. One swings a club. Some are nude. Others wear butcher aprons. They march. I expect to see fire. I expect to see a beast chained and spitting. My breath is hot. The scent of urine stings the air. I'm trying to keep to the contract, the one you posted to the motel room before we left—to keep things to myself, what comes out of the body, what moves inside it, what I want. I descend the trail, crouching in the shade. I remove the vials. I hammer in the spile to catch what will rise. Eventually you join me, the hour when the birds have begun to loop through the air. *Raptors*, you say and, *We can't camp here*. I watch the birds, their gripping dance. *They can't be mated pairs*, I say and lean towards the spout to suckle.

Here is another example:

Two Shapes Mirrored
by Tina Barry

The lights of a Ferris wheel blink to the hurried tune of a heart. A young couple shares a seat, the man bent forward, rocking. The loom of his shadow reminds the woman of a test in elementary school: two shapes mirrored right and left. She felt silly answering, "Butterfly?" She doesn't trust slippers. Prefers the disruption of heels on hard floors. A silhouette bumps and glitters; someone's history better left unknown. The word "medium" means an apartment roof with no railing, the White Cliffs of Dover, a question asked by an agitated foreigner. *What?* she'd say. *What?* Staring into his mouth like a long passage home.

CHAPTER 25

Writing two more drafts

IMAGINE WHERE ONE OF YOUR childhood friends is now. Imagine where your old t-shirt that you donated to a clothing drive is now. Imagine where those love letters went after you threw them in the trash.

Where are they now? Where did they go? What happened?

For example: "What happened to that man whose eyes held my gaze in that New York café? Who was he? Where is he now? What is he doing now?"

CHOOSE TWO OR MORE OF THE FOLLOWING PROMPTS AND WRITE TWO DRAFTS OF A PROSE POEM:
Write a prose poem or two in response to the above question of "where is he/she/it now?" Let the question lead you into the writing.
   Or
Write a response to:
The scent of roses brought back that early memory of …

What was that early memory? Tell the whole truth. How did it make you feel? What images do you see in your head when recalling the scene? Did you include them? Include them!

Or

A letter comes in the mail. What does it say? Did you win the lottery or did your lover write to say goodbye?

Write a response to that letter.

Write what you love. Write with passion and the voice will sing through the poem.

Prose poems are about stirring an emotional response in the reader. To do that, the poet must honestly care about the subject of the poem and want to communicate to others so they too will care or at least be interested.

CHAPTER 26

Language

PROSODY IS THE STUDY OF the mechanisms that create rhythm or sound in poetry. Language, grammar, punctuation, pauses, white space, the poem's shape, ellipses, imagery, description, and the incorporation of poetic devices or elements provide an overall "feel" or music to the poem. When you analyze or examine your poems or the samples in this text, you are studying the fibers that woven together make up the whole tapestry of the prose poem.

POETIC LANGUAGE

Poetic language and poetic devices should be colorful and meaningful. Poets learn to use special language skills. We have studied several of these in this text. Here is a review:

a. **Imagery:** The basic cornerstone of any poetry is the image, a phrase or word that conveys a mental image or an emotion to the reader. For example, take the sentence "Death comes to me with soft fingers." The image often crosses over into symbolism for some readers. (Would most people associate death with soft fingers?) This is not only an image, a surprisingly "different" one, but also **personification (the**

humanizing of an object) because death is given a human trait: soft fingers.

b. **Metaphor:** For example, "All the world's a stage." This says the whole world is a theater. From some perspectives, we can perceive that as true!

c. **Simile: a comparison between two things,** when something is said to be "like," or to resemble, something else. For example, "The human brain has two halves, divided like a kernel of walnut."

d. **Repetition** (also known as "anaphora," which is repetition with variation): Repetition is one of my favorite poetic devices. Revisit the sample poems I have included and enjoy the rhythm and impact of repetition. One word of caution: Don't overdo repetition or it might come across as comical. Repetition connects our inner selves with our rhythmic heartbeat and circadian rhythms we live with daily. Think about the nursery rhyme or the hypnotic rhythm of a chant. Not everything should be a nursery rhyme or a chant, but sometimes repetition is just right.

The crucial aspect of writing prose poetry is that the poem must have structure, which is the frame upon which the poem is built, the sentences and the punctuation. The structure will include rhythm and will be filled in with well-written, well-placed, meaningful language.

Analyze a poem you like or one you have written and write a list of each element or technique that the poet has used to provide an overall effect or emotional trigger.

CHAPTER 27

Minimalism and Compression

MINIMALISM MEANS TO WRITE WHAT needs to be said with the fewest possible words. It means cutting those words that do not add to the overall meaning of the poem.

"Tight writing" means lines or prose written with the utmost consideration for the weight and meaning of each word, keeping the poem simple but powerful, crisp and clean. Therefore, make strong word choices, focusing on the nouns and verbs, and reduce adjectives and adverbs.

Compression refers to the main elements staying compressed or small. For example, a compressed prose poem might consist of three lines with a minimal choice of sparse words. It might describe a tiny anecdote or event. Compression occurs more often in prose poetry and flash stories than in other creative writing. Some might argue that the complete elimination of articles and conjunctions in poetry might fall within the parameters of experimental and contemporary poetry; however, cutting pronouns and unnecessary words can at times create a powerful poem.

For example, read the following prose poem. Later we'll eliminate most of the indefinite, definite articles and conjunctions for comparison:

The Linear and Circular One Sentence of Tattoo Designs over His Body

Compare the following versions of the same poem:

David runs through Goliath with a sword but Goliath stands strong, his sandal strap broken by the tip of steel, blood at the ankle, a few hairs shaved from his knee, but he stays upright, an angel of the bottomless pit, the hero of one tattooed story with its swirly blue ink marks connecting letters over each vertebra, letters that spell out "Never again" and "violence is not the way" with the word "way" spiraling down the spinal column, each lumbar protrusion covered with inky lines and letters, until the ink bleeds into Popeye opening a can of worms on the left buttock, and Olive smoking a pipe on the right buttock, the pipe smoke weaving a curly-Q whirly loop and merging into Spiderman's web on the left thigh, the web webbing its lacey stars and stripes network down and around the shins, around and around until it splatters inky blue spiders over the gastrocnemius of the left calf muscle and covers the ankles and feet with tiny Buddhas that continue under the feet and protect the soles of feet and the soul of the man, (but how did he suffer through that painful tattooing?) and seen from under jeans, the feet appear dirty and garden-weary but when rolled up, like Eliot's Prufrock on the beach, the design works magic like a waterfall works magic, a watershed of rainbow colors spreading in a rainfall of tattoo etchings across his massive shoulders, his sharp abs, pecs, scapulae, triceps, biceps, quadriceps, embellishing and fertilizing all six hundred and thirty-nine muscles, a landscape of linked vessels and lines emerging whenever he takes off his shirt, a rare occurrence, only when the gorgeous and the giants come to town and he dreads the time when he runs out of tattoo space on his skin and he must share his stories with his words instead.

REWRITTEN WITH ELIMINATIONS:

David runs his sword through Goliath but the giant stands strong, sandal strap broken by steel-tip, ankle bleeding, hairs shaved from knees, he stays upright, angel of bottomless pits, hero of one tattooed story, its swirly blue ink marks connecting letters over each vertebra, letters that spell "Never again... violence is not the way" with "way" spiraling down his spinal column, each lumbar protrusion covered, inky letters, bleeding into Popeye opening one can of worms on two buttocks, Olive smoking her pipe, pipe smoke weaving curly-Q whirly loops around and down, merging into Spiderman's web on his left thigh, webbing lacey stars, stripes down, around shins, around, around until it splatters inky blue spiders over his gastrocnemius, his left calf muscle, covers ankles, feet, with tiny Buddhas under feet, protecting soles, protecting his soul, (but how on earth did he suffer through that painful tattooing?) seen from under jeans, feet appear dirty, garden-weary, when rolled up, like Eliot's Prufrock trousers, works magic like waterfalls work magic, rainbow color watershed raining tattoo etchings across massive shoulders, sharp abs, pecs, scapulae, triceps, biceps, quadriceps, embellishing, fertilizing all six hundred-thirty-nine muscles into linked vessels, maps, lines emerging whenever he takes off his shirt, rare however, only when gorgeous giants come to town, when he dreads running out of tattoo space, when he must share stories with words instead.

The rewrite demonstrates a piece written without conjunctions or articles, in one long sentence, with a faster pacing that speeds right along. That's great when writing about a mountain bike speeding down the rocky mountain trail, but not when writing about a leopard on the hunt or a tattoo that squiggles and draws patterns over a human body. With the leopard on the hunt, the poem's pace might speed up and slow down, as the leopard stalks its prey, waits, runs to catch up, watches, pounces, and so on.

CHAPTER 28

Types of prose poems

I HAVE LISTED BELOW SEVERAL of my favorite styles or poetic strategies that work well when writing prose poetry. These are but a few of the infinite options and certainly only limited by the writer's imagination.

a. **The rant**: Does your prose poem complain or rave with anger but without justification? No editor or reader wants to read a paragraph or even a line of complaining unless there is an underlying sense of truth with or without a sense of humor. Be careful when writing a rant. Beginning writers tend to ramble with this form.

b. **A *"poem of witness"*** documents in poetic language events or people that the world needs to see or hear about. Carolyn Forché's prose poem "The Colonel" is an excellent example.

c. **Ekphrastic:** When one writes a response to a work of art or to music, or to an object such as an urn or sculpture, this is an "ekphrastic" response poem. It is fun to look at a painting and draft a poem about what you see.

d. **The List poem.** This is one of my favorite forms. Here is an example by Sheryl Clough.

Seven Ways of Looking at a Red Wheelbarrow

One

In pieces on my deck. Assembly chart has blown away, over the bay.

Two

A poem yet unwritten. Stare at the blank page.

Three

An ungainly bird, flying upside down, wooden handles thrust ahead to break air currents.

Four

A home for robins. More solid than the fan vent they built on last year.

Five

Raccoon hideout: at five a.m. fat mother and four offspring peer around the barrow's metal edge.

Six

Holder for falling leaves. I rake, more blow down, I rake faster.

Seven

Beagle bathtub: my daughter's dog has rolled in dead fish, again.

e. **Letters or epistolary poems:** These are poems written as if they were a message to a person or a group.
f. **Surreal and fabulist:** fables, myth, magical thinking, fairy tales. These all make great prose poems. Below is a section of Laura Madeline Wiseman's prose poem "Under the Frankincense Trees," an example of magical thinking with a fairy tale quality.

There are trolls behind us. *Don't, you say.* I obey, refusing to turn around. I check my airflow, tap my chest computer, increase the volume on my headset. The only thing to hear is wind. There are trolls under Australian bridges, trolls on US highways, trolls in the tunnels of Russia. In Sochi, they gripped the gates, slammed fists into vendor doors, pushed fingertips through manhole covers. In Moscow, they whispered something like *Kozels, kozels, kozels.* When we climbed Sydney Harbor Bridge in our jumpsuits, tubes pulling in the wind, our facemasks less a facemask than a shield against the spray, you said: *This bridge isn't going to survive the waves.* The amphitheater was gone, the aquarium, the gardens…I walk ahead into the burn.

Or look at the following pieces extracted from *When Songbirds Take Flight* by Shannon Nakai, a tiny makeover of the story of Dorothy from *The Wizard of Oz* in prose poem form:

The farmhouse, September 20, 1913, Elk County, KS

Dorothy presses her wide barreled thumbs along the fluted rims of piecrust. Her eyes the color of rain follow the grease-smocked recipe. She sprinkles fistfuls of flour onto the counter. Outside Aunt Em scatters seeds for the chickens, watching the girls in the window frame. Her gaze follows Dorothy in the mornings when she wanders from room to room filling the vases with milkweeds and goldenrods.

Once Dorothy disappeared for an entire day. Em found her starry-eyed on her back in a soy field, babbling about a faraway place…

She insists the faraway place is real, she insists that she is going back, restless in the real world, which she now calls the dream world, ready, she says, to wake up again.

g. **Metaphorical poem**: Russell Edson's poetry takes an image and extends it into an extraordinary rendition of that image. For example, Edson's prose poem "The Rat's Tight Schedule."

See the list of references and links at the end of this book. There are some terrific examples of prose poems and greater detail for delving into these strategies and many others.

CHALLENGE:

Choose one of the above strategies and write a prose poem. Write quickly with abandon and without editing. You can clean it up later. Put on the timer for fifteen minutes. Shut the door. Silence the phone. Now write.

Or

Write a prose poem about a "hot pink tutu." What if you woke up wearing one? What if it had legs of its own? What if it was a required school uniform?

CHAPTER 29

Ways to write fresh poems

- Here are some examples of tired old themes. You can write about them, but understand that so many poets have written about these themes, that editors are tired of them.
  - mommy dearest
  - childhood abuse
  - your surgery
  - his cancer
  - your life growing up on a farm. Unless you grew up in a tree-house on a deserted island or were the son or daughter of a mobster, your life story might be too like other life stories to be of interest. You can, however, write about places, things, and eras, with the focus on the place, thing, or era.
  - love lost
  - how your lover is wonderful
  - how your ex is awful
  - dreams or anything to do with dreams; don't even use the word "dream."

Here are some examples of clichés or worn-out phrases:

"Every fiber of my being" "God give me strength" "Hear my cry" "the pregnant moon"
"walking on eggshells" "over the moon in love" "sunny disposition" "ruby red lips"
"Eyes blue as the sky" or a "love deep as the ocean."

If you want to publish your poems, don't send magazines poems about mommy dearest, alcoholic Dad or abusive brother unless these poems come from an interesting or unusual angle.

Browse prose poems on the Internet or in books and find themes that appear fresh and appealing. What do you think was so appealing that an editor chose to publish them?

Joining a poetry class or a writing workshop group is a great way to find out whether your poems appeal and have a fresh approach.

Use the references in this book's resource list and read as many prose poems as you can.

Read books about prose poetry.

Stay aware of those topics that appeal to you and which poems grab you.

Whenever you travel, take a notebook and pencil and jot down ideas as they come to you. Sometimes, unusual anecdotes or events can make for playful writing later.

Taking a course in prose poems or short stories can inspire you to write. Either an online or in-person course can be lots of fun.

CHAPTER 30

More tips...

❧ MOOD

A POEM CAN SET A mood. Mood is a state of mind or feeling. The sensory information and poetic language used by the writer sets up the reader to feel a certain way.

❧ THEME

Stay away from mundane themes such as a walk in the park or a sailboat at sunset, unless that walk or sail approaches the theme from an unusual angle. Stay away from describing the dreams you have at night. The reader cannot relate to your dreams.

❧ THE POET'S VOICE

Each poet has a unique style or sound. This is called the poet's voice. Just as you listen to a song on the radio and can identify the singer, so it is with poems. When experience and writing skill finally weave together, the poet commands a unique tapestry that is his or her "voice." Your voice will develop over time with practice.

❦ SUBTEXT/IMPLICATION

What on earth is subtext?

A prose poem can work on more than one level, just as a story often has a subplot.

Subtext lies beneath the lines, implies that other things are going on in the poem, and these come through to the reader. Subtext paints a subtle picture without telling the reader what to visualize or what the poet might also refer to in his/her poem, such as symbolism.

For example, let's say the narrator of the poem speaks of a thumbprint found on a yellowed page in a book. The resulting poem about whom this print might have belonged to might give rise to feelings of loneliness or desperation. None of us can escape human emotions, and these make us human. The poet does not tell us what to think or how to feel but sets the mood for the reader via specific language and how the poet uses this language. Readers with different backgrounds will perhaps read different emotions into a poem. Thus, response to and interpretation of poems stays subjective and individual.

CHAPTER 31

Mastering the prose poem

PRACTICE, TAKE A COURSE, AND read prose poetry. Can't find any classes, or any prose poetry? Ask a librarian.

<u>Options:</u>

- Local community colleges
- The local writers' community or organization
- Online courses such as those at Gotham in New York or WritersDigest.com
- Read the resource list at the end of this book
- Write and do the prompts and exercises in the book
- Place a giant wall calendar on your wall and write in how much you wrote that day. Leave no day blank.
- Read the chapter in this book about workshop groups.

AN IMPORTANT EXERCISE IN MASTERING THE PROSE POEM FOLLOWS:

Print and read a prose poem or one of the pieces you have written and stay aware of how it makes you feel. Examine the piece closely and highlight the words or devices (poetic tricks or language) that made you feel this way.

When describing the emotions raised by the poem, elaborate on the feelings. For example, instead of the "poem made me feel sad," describe that feeling in more depth. "It made me feel sad because that happened to me when I was a child." Or "I could smell the pine needles my father used for the campfire." Or "I could visualize that little girl in her white lace dress and black patent shoes."

CHAPTER 32

C.O.A.P.

C.O.A.P. IS AN ACRONYM REFERRING to the four keys to revision, which are:

1. **Cut**
2. **Organize**
3. **Add**
4. **Polish**

1. **Cutting** is deleting whole unnecessary words or "filler" words not related to the point or message of your prose poem.

    The second sentence below cuts unnecessary and clichéd words from the first sentence.

    * Johnny sprinted quickly to reach the morning express fast train which traveled faster than a speeding bullet to his destination in way less than an hour.
    * Johnny sprinted to reach the morning express train which traveled to his destination in less than one hour.

2. **Organize** refers to logical idea progression and unity of the whole poem. Does your poem build a picture or a feeling and offer more and more with every sentence? That is your goal. Keep working on it.

3. **Add:** Sometimes during revision, worried about "the rules," poets "cut" or "trim" a poem so closely that they drain all the life and texture out of the poem. Sometimes a poem doesn't seem finished even to the poet. It does not reach a conclusion or a high level of drama, description or emotion. Add to the poem whatever you think it needs. Or write another poem.

4. **Polish:** Write multiple drafts and **hone** each one. Check for consistency in point of view, tense, clarity and verb usage. Check for correct punctuation in sentences and review for awkward words or excess detail, explanation or backstory, excess use of word modifiers such as adverbs and adjectives, excess dialogue and unwieldy writing.

Some poems simply aren't successful no matter how much you work on them. It might be that the idea behind the poem is too complicated, or you feel too shy to write a truly honest poem, or you don't yet have the writing skill to have the poem clearly say what you want it to say, or it just doesn't communicate to other people. Put the unsuccessful poem aside and start a new one. You have an infinite well of creativity!

REVIEW:
Review the poems you have written from the prompts.

Use the following reminders to evaluate each poem:

* The title. Does it relate to the rest of the poem? Remember, it is the first hook for the reader.
* Do the first few lines of the poem also hook in the reader?
* Read it aloud. Does it drag, sound awkward, go too quickly or too slowly?

- Does it evoke a picture in the reader's mind?
- Read through and circle clichés, adverbs and adjectives. Can you eliminate any of these?
- Does the poem make sense? Is it meaningful?
- Check the spelling and grammar for mistakes or typos.
- Do the last few lines offer a satisfying ending?

CHAPTER 33

How do I know whether my poem is good?

WHEN REVIEWING YOUR POEMS, CHECK the following list and make sure you have worked within these guidelines. After you have completed the previous C.O.A.P. chapter and rewritten your work according to the suggestions in that chapter, it is time to do the final review.

Here are some mistakes I find that many poets make when submitting to our journal. Look at your final drafts and review and correct any of these:

- A loss of focus on the theme or purpose of the poem
- Use of clichés and unoriginal themes
- Use of passive voice (Once is enough.)
- Excessive use of adverbs (One or two is enough.)
- Not enough strong verbs (**active**). Instead there are too many **verbs from the "to be" family**:

"I **had to have** that bag. I **should have been given** it for my birthday." (Weak.)

"I **wanted** that bag for my birthday. I wish they had given it to me." (Stronger.)

Another example: "John **was** always **chosen** every year by the class **to be** the clown." (Weak.)

"Every year, the class **chose** John as the clown." (Stronger.)

* **Verbosity** and rambling. Keep it direct and keep it tight. Use concrete specifics. Write what you mean.
* Boring or generic **titles.**
* **Lack of creativity** with themes, titles and presentation.
* Spelling **errors**. Read and reread, and have someone else read to catch any errors.
* **Mixing** up points of view, which offers an awkward read. If the poem starts out in first person, keep it that way. Don't jump into third person halfway through.
* **Tense inconsistencies:** Keep tense consistent. If you are in present tense, keep it in present tense.
* **Writing about dreams.** This is a tired old way to write and most readers don't relate to others' dreams.
* Writers make a mistake by sending poems to journals without first **reading the journal's guidelines.**

Above all else, a great way to improve one's writing is through a poetry course, online or in person. Sometimes these courses or groups are called "writing workshops."

CHAPTER 34

Workshop groups

AFTER YOU BELIEVE YOUR POEM is finally finished, it is time to have other people read it and give you feedback. The best way to get constructive feedback on your poems is to join a writers' group whose members trade their drafts, read them, discuss them as a group, share what they like about your work, and suggest improvements. There are many online groups. Contact your local writers' organization or form your own group.

How do you know if your poem is meaningful or needs work? Make sure you form an honest writers' group. They should all be writers who will support your growth as a poet with suggestions for strengthening or improvement, and not vague comments such as "I love this poem" or "I hate this poem." (Yes, someone did say that to me about a poem.) If you feel unable or unwilling to hear from other writers that your work ought to be revised, tightened or improved so it better communicates to readers, you are not ready to belong to a workshop group.

If we expect tact and honesty, we need to give others the same. When critiquing other works, offer **three** examples of what works well for the poem before offering **three** suggestions for improvement. In my early days in the master of fine arts in creative writing program, I felt my insides collapse at times during the workshop groups. People had suggestions for work I had thought was perfect! I listened to and tried their suggestions, and some of them really helped me, or inspired another poem. Do listen, even if it's hard at first. Somebody might come up with a great new title for your poem, or point out how your work is improving.

Now that I am a seasoned writer, a comment that sounds like "I hate your poem" slides off my skin, but writers who deliver opinions without giving the reasons behind them have no place in any group. At the beginning of the session, set the guidelines about diplomacy and supportive honesty. A writer who tells you he/she "loves your poem" without explaining why is not doing you any favors. He or she should accompany the comment with two or three reasons. Ask him or her, "What did you like or love about the poem?"

Many writers are uncomfortable with prose poems and workshop groups focusing exclusively on prose poems are few. Create one yourself.

Or if it's more convenient, join an online workshop group. Google "online critique groups prose poems" and several sites come up. Alternatively, take a course or an online course at the myriad online writing schools. Read the reviews of these programs before enrolling to find the one that is right for you. When learning to write, I took courses with Gotham Writers Workshop Online. Another excellent program (expensive) for online non-degree learning is Stanford University's online learning program.

CHAPTER 35

Lots more tips...

WHAT I LOOK FOR IN SUBMISSIONS OF PROSE POETRY AS AN EDITOR WITH *THE BACOPA LITERARY REVIEW:*

a. Clear and concise poems
b. Originality. A theme approached from a fresh angle.
c. A satisfactory ending.
d. Logical progression towards an end.
e. Creativity and original thought.
f. The poet's unique understanding of truth or reality.
g. Consistency.
h. Perfect spelling and grammar that makes sense.
i. Concrete specifics that offer the reader images.
j. Language that appeals to the senses.
k. Rhythm and musicality achieved through punctuation and language.
l. A writing style that combines all the elements discussed in this text and results in a poet's unique "voice." Acquiring your personal "voice" takes practice and experience. For example, the voice of well-known prose poet Russell Edson is easy to recognize because it is uniquely his own. Beginners, don't worry about your poetic "voice," because it will come on its own after you have been writing for a while.

m. Keep backstory to a minimum. "Backstory" refers to what happened before the scene you are describing in the poem. Written at a minimum and with concision it might work, but unless you are a skilled poet, stay away from explaining what happened before the poem started. Start in the action of the scene, but orient the reader to the scene's time or place very soon after starting the poem.

HERE IS AN EXAMPLE:

"Staring ahead **like** an actor frozen on stage, a **white-haired woman sits** on **a porch in twilight**, red chair creaking, **rocking**, rocking."

In the above example, we are oriented to who, what, where and when. We even get a simile. The details orient the reader to place and time of day.

CONCLUSION

I HOPE YOU HAVE ENJOYED working through this little book of 35 tips for writing powerful prose poems. I enjoyed the process of putting together my teaching and lecture materials. Watch for the next book in the *35 Tips* series. **Happy writing, and remember, master the rules before you bend them.**

Poems or excerpts of poems included by *The Bacopa Literary Review* 2016 authors in alphabetical order by last name:

Tina Barry   "Two Shapes Mirrored"
Sheryl Clough   "Seven Ways of Looking at a Red
                                         Wheelbarrow"
Kaye Linden   "The Linear and Circular One Sentence
                                         of Tattoo Designs Over His Body"
                                         "The Wet"
Leslie Anne Mcilroy   "Big Bang"
Shannon Nakai   "When Songbirds Take Flight"
Marian Shapiro   "Non-sense"
Jacob Trask   "Splintered"
Laura Madeline Wiseman   "Under the Frankincense Trees"

RESOURCE LIST

The Bacopa Literary Review. Gainesville: Writers Alliance, 2016. Print.

Alderson, Martha. *The Plot Whisperer Book of Writing Prompts: Easy Exercises to Get You Writing.* Avon, MA: Adams Media, 2013. Print.

Barnstone, Aliki, and Willis Barnstone. *A Book of Women Poets from Antiquity to Now.* n.p., n.d. Print.

Bernays, Anne, and Pamela Painter. *What If? Writing Exercises for Fiction Writers.* Boston: Longman, 2010. Print.

Bishop, Wendy. *Thirteen Ways of Looking for a Poem: A Guide to Writing Poetry.* New York: Longman, 2000. Print.

Bookeval.com (author support services)

Clements, Brian, and Jamey Dunham. *An Introduction to the Prose Poem.* Danbury, CT: Firewheel Editions, 2009. Print.

Edson, Russell. *The Tunnel: Selected Poems.* Oberlin, OH: Oberlin College, 1994. Print.

Finch, Annie, and Kathrine Varnes. *An Exaltation of Forms: Contemporary Poets Celebrate the Diversity of Their Art.* Ann Arbor: U of Michigan, 2002. Print.

Forché, Carolyn. "The Colonel." *Poetry Foundation.* https://www. poetryfoundation.org/poems-and-poets/poems/detail/49862. Poetry Foundation, n.d. Retrieved 15 Apr. 2017.

Friebert, Stuart, and David Young. *Models of the Universe: An Anthology of the Prose Poem.* Oberlin, OH: Oberlin College, 1995. Print.

Hirsch, Edward. *A Poet's Glossary.* Boston: Houghton Mifflin Harcourt, 2014. Print.

Hodges, John C. (John Cunyus). *Hodges' Harbrace Handbook.* Fort Worth: Harcourt College, 2001. Print.

Lehman, David. *Great American Prose Poems: From Poe to the Present.* New York: Scribner Poetry, 2003. Print.

Linden, Kaye. *35 Tips for Writing a Brilliant Flash Story.* CreateSpace, 2015. Print.

McDowell, Gary L., and F. Daniel Rzicznek. *The Rose Metal Press Field Guide to Prose Poetry: Contemporary Poets in Discussion and Practice.* Brookline, MA: Rose Metal, 2010. Print

Packard, William. *The Poet's Dictionary: A Handbook of Prosody and Poetic Devices.* New York.: Harper & Row, 1991. Print.

Wilbers, Steven. *Keys to Great Writing.* Cincinnati: Writer's Digest, 2000. Print.

"I have a dream," a speech delivered by Dr. Martin Luther King, Jr., on August 28, 1963 at Washington, D.C. YouTube: *https://www. youtube.com/watch?v=HRIF4_WzU1w*

www.writersalliance.org

www.kayelinden.com

ABOUT THE AUTHOR

KAYE LINDEN, BORN AND RAISED in Sydney, Australia, is a registered nurse with an MFA in fiction, now studying for another MFA in prose poetry. She is past and current poetry and short story editor of *The Bacopa Literary Review*, a former teacher of short stories and prose poetry at Santa Fe College in Gainesville, Florida, assistant editor for *Soundings Review*, previous judge for *Spark Anthology*, and past and current medical editor for *"Present e-learning Systems."* She writes in all genres but especially loves prose poetry. Kaye has three grown sons and lives on five acres in a renovated farmhouse with her husband and three dogs. Her hobbies include gardening and making real Australian brewed tea in a teapot.

Kaye's publications are extensive and include honors and awards. Visit her at www.kayelinden.com and sign up to follow her blog.

Made in the USA
Las Vegas, NV
22 November 2024

12420124R00066